A TRUE BOOK™

The Sioux

**KEVIN CUNNINGHAM
AND PETER BENOIT**

Children's Press®
An Imprint of Scholastic Inc.
New York Toronto London Auckland Sydney
Mexico City New Delhi Hong Kong
Danbury, Connecticut

Content Consultant
Scott Manning Stevens, PhD
Director, McNickle Center
Newberry Library
Chicago, Illinois

Library of Congress Cataloging-in-Publication Data

Cunningham, Kevin, 1966–
   The Sioux/Kevin Cunningham and Peter Benoit.
      p. cm.—(A true book)
   Includes bibliographical references and index.
   ISBN-13: 978-0-531-20768-0 (lib. bdg.)   978-0-531-29310-2 (pbk.)
   ISBN-10: 0-531-20768-4 (lib. bdg.)   0-531-29310-6 (pbk.)
   1. Dakota Indians—Juvenile literature. I. Benoit, Peter, 1955– II. Title. III. Series.
   E99.D1C86 2011
   978.004'975244—dc22   2010049083

All rights reserved. Published in 2011 by Children's Press, an imprint of Scholastic Inc.
Printed in China 62
SCHOLASTIC, CHILDREN'S PRESS, A TRUE BOOK and associated logos are trademarks and/or registered trademarks of Scholastic Inc.

2 3 4 5 6 7 8 9 10 R 19 18 17 16 15 14 13 12

Find the Truth!

Everything you are about to read is true *except* for one of the sentences on this page.

Which one is **TRUE**?

T or F The Sioux believed the shirt they wore in the Ghost Dance turned away bullets.

T or F The Sioux never encountered the Lewis and Clark expedition.

Find the answers in this book.

Contents

THE **BIG** TRUTH!

The Battle of the Greasy Grass

4 How the Sioux Lived

Teepee

Sioux women
turned bison
hides into usable
cloth called
"buffalo robes."

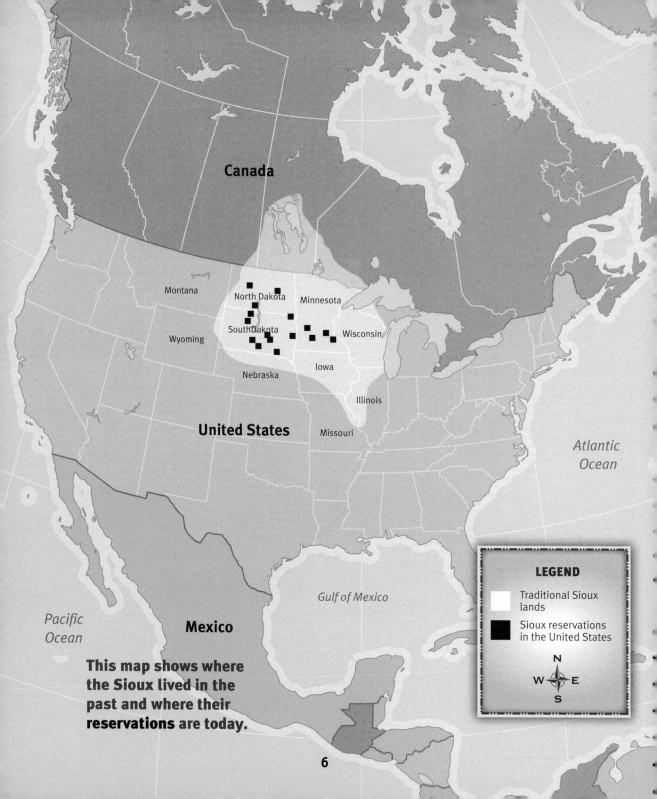

Canada

Montana

North Dakota Minnesota

SouthDakota Wisconsin

Wyoming

Nebraska Iowa

Illinois

United States Missouri

Atlantic Ocean

Pacific Ocean

Mexico

Gulf of Mexico

This map shows where the Sioux lived in the past and where their reservations are today.

LEGEND

Traditional Sioux lands

Sioux reservations in the United States

N
W   E
S

CHAPTER 1

Beginnings

The Sioux once lived near the Great Lakes. They were divided into three groups—the Lakota, the Dakota, and the Nakota—based on which language they spoke. They hunted and fished for meat. To add to their food supply, they also farmed fields of what Native Americans called the Three Sisters—maize (corn), beans, and squash. During the 1600s, however, other Indian groups pushed west and forced out the Sioux. The Sioux began to **migrate** in search of a new place to live.

← *Sioux is an Ojibwe word meaning "little snakes."*

The Sioux sometimes caught wild horses.

The Horse Changes Everything

On the Great Plains to the west, the Cheyenne and Comanche had begun to use horses. No horses lived in the Americas before Christopher Columbus brought a few on his second voyage, in 1493. After that, Spanish explorers and settlers continued to bring the animals. They traded some to Native Americans. Soon, peoples such as the Comanche, the Apache, and others began hunting on horseback across large territories.

The horse offered many advantages. Unlike the dogs Plains peoples had raised before, the horse ate grass instead of meat. A horse was stronger and could haul more than a dog pulling a sled. The horse also allowed people to travel farther and faster in search of food such as bison (buffalo). Around 1730, the Cheyenne began to trade with the Sioux. Once the Sioux had bought horses, they joined other Plains peoples as horse-riding **nomads**.

Dogs and horses pulled a sled called a travois (tra-VOY).

A travois could move over soft ground and snow more easily than a cart with wheels could.

Water carved the fantastic shapes of the peaks in the Badlands.

Three Sioux ride through the rugged Badlands region in western South Dakota.

The Black Hills

The Lakota migrated west as far as the Missouri River in what is now South Dakota. The Dakota Sioux mainly lived farther east, in Minnesota. There, powerful peoples such as the Hidatsa and the Mandan stopped the Lakota from crossing the river. In the mid-1700s, smallpox and other European diseases swept the Great Plains. The Lakota escaped the disease and drove away the weakened Cheyenne. Soon after, the Lakota rode into the Black Hills, a wooded mountain range surrounded by grassy plains.

The Great Pox

Smallpox is a deadly disease that causes the body to break out in painful blisters. Those who survive often have permanent scars. Smallpox probably arrived in Mexico with the Spanish in 1520. From then on, more native people in the Americas may have died from this disease than from any other event. Why? Native Americans had never been in contact with this disease before. Their bodies could not fight it off, so when smallpox hit, it hit hard. Often, 80 to 90 percent of the victims died.

Smallpox killed millions of Indians across North America.

Lewis and Clark first met the Sioux near what is now Pierre, South Dakota.

CHAPTER 2

The First Meeting

The Sioux had their first meeting with American explorers in late August 1804. The expedition of Meriwether Lewis and William Clark traveled up the Missouri River as part of its mission to explore the massive Louisiana Territory. On the way, the Sioux refused to allow the explorers to pass. Until, that is, the expedition prepared to fight. Both sides backed off. The expedition passed by but noted the Sioux's **hostile** actions.

⬅ The United States paid France about $15 million for the Louisiana Territory.

Clashes With Settlers

For the first part of the 1800s, the Sioux and the United States remained at peace. Starting in the mid-1830s, however, American settlers began traveling westward along the Oregon Trail. On the way, they crossed land claimed by the Sioux and other Indian tribes. The Indians considered them trespassers. Warriors mounted on horses began to make lightning-fast raids against settlers. Fighting with both settlers and U.S. Army **cavalry** became more common.

The territories crossed by the Oregon Trail and the Lewis and Clark expedition include many of today's western states.

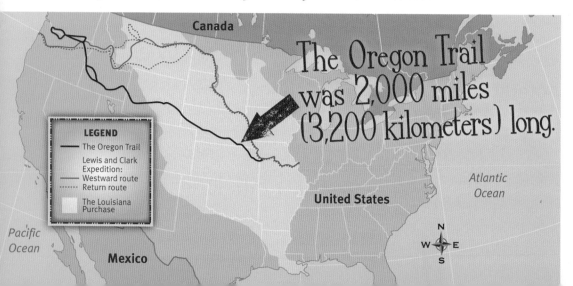

The Oregon Trail was 2,000 miles (3,200 kilometers) long.

Canada

LEGEND
— The Oregon Trail
Lewis and Clark Expedition:
— Westward route
⋯⋯ Return route
☐ The Louisiana Purchase

United States

Atlantic Ocean

Pacific Ocean

Mexico

N W E S

The Sioux often camped near Fort Laramie in Wyoming.

A Short Time of Peace

In 1851, U.S. government officials asked the Sioux and several other peoples for talks to stop the violence. Both sides signed the Fort Laramie **Treaty**. It recognized the Sioux's rights to their lands in return for the Sioux allowing settlers to pass safely. The United States also agreed to pay $50,000 per year for 50 years for permission to build forts and roads on lands belonging to the Sioux and others.

Violence Returns

The deal soon fell apart. Bad feelings returned in August 1854 when a U.S. Army officer named John L. Grattan attacked a Sioux camp near Fort Laramie over an incident involving a dead cow. Grattan had wanted a fight. He got one. The Sioux wiped out his entire 30-man force. On September 3, 1855, General William Harney took revenge by killing more than 100 Sioux men, women, and children.

U.S. Army troops traveled across the Plains to fight Native Americans.

About 100,000 gold seekers moved to Colorado in 1859. ➡️

Miners dug deep into the mountains to find gold and silver.

Gold Rush!

In 1859, the discovery of gold in Colorado brought a new flood of miners and settlers. The United States refused to stop the gold rush. It also never paid some of the people who were promised money in the treaty. The Sioux needed the payments for food after a drought killed local crops. At one point, a Sioux spokesman in Minnesota asked if he could buy food on credit for his people. An official is said to have replied, "So far as I am concerned, if they are hungry, let them eat grass."

The Sioux renewed their attacks on settlers and miners. The U.S. Army moved in to stop them. In 1862, the short Dakota War ended with 38 Sioux being executed as prisoners of war. Fighting continued throughout Minnesota and the Dakotas. The war showed signs of ending after the Battle of Killdeer Mountain in July 1864. The Sioux had suffered heavy losses. In 1868, the Sioux signed a new treaty at Fort Laramie.

Native Americans meet with U.S. government officials to sign the Fort Laramie Treaty of 1868.

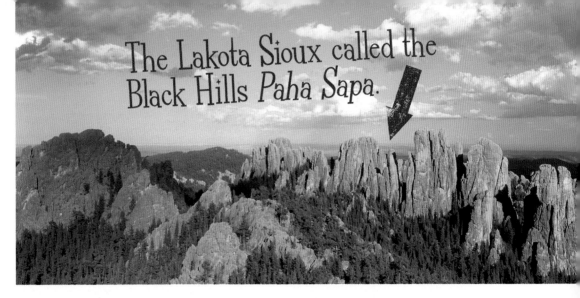

The Lakota Sioux called the Black Hills *Paha Sapa*.

The Black Hills boast the tallest peaks in North America east of the Rocky Mountains.

The Black Hills

The treaty promised the Sioux control of the Black Hills, a land **sacred** to them. They believe the Great Spirit lives there. The Sioux opposed mining in the Black Hills and thought the treaty would end it. But U.S. Army cavalry led by George A. Custer rode into the Black Hills in 1874 to investigate rumors of gold. Miners soon rushed into the hills. The Sioux, angry over the treaty being ignored, attacked the miners. The Great Sioux War had begun.

The Sioux do battle on horseback.

CHAPTER 3

From Bad to Worse

The Sioux proved to be tougher than the U.S. Army believed. After a number of small battles and chases during 1875, the war continued. The U.S. Army then tried to strike in winter, when the Sioux and their allies were weakest. But the plan failed. On June 17, 1876, a U.S. Army force of more than 1,300 men escaped a surprise attack by Sioux and Northern Cheyenne warriors at Rosebud Creek and had to retreat.

← The Great Sioux War is sometimes called the Black Hills War.

The battle is also known as Custer's Last Stand.

Little Bighorn

A more famous battle took place eight days later. The Native American defeat of U.S. Army forces at the Battle of the Little Bighorn was the Sioux's greatest victory. The Sioux remember

George A. Custer was the leader of the U.S. Army troops at the Battle of the Little Bighorn. He was killed in the fight.

it as the Battle of the Greasy Grass. News of the battle reached Washington, D.C., as the nation celebrated its 100-year anniversary. The government, stunned, rallied more troops. Their plan: defeat the Indians for good.

Defeat

The Sioux did not have enough men to hunt, fight, and protect non-warriors such as children and old people at the same time. Throughout 1876, U.S. Army troops defeated the Sioux and their allies in a string of battles. Most Sioux ended up on reservations—unwanted land watched by the government. In 1877, they signed away the Black Hills to the U.S. government. Though some Sioux fought on, the war was lost.

A Sioux girl sits in front of a teepee on a reservation in western South Dakota.

The Battle of the Greasy Grass

Sitting Bull

The holy man and leader Tatanka Iyotake, or Sitting Bull, had a vision of U.S. soldiers falling like grasshoppers.

On June 25, 1876, George Custer led the U.S. Seventh Cavalry to the Greasy Grass Creek near Montana's Little Bighorn River. There, his scouts spotted a camp of Sioux, Northern Cheyenne, and Arapaho. Unaware of the enemy's numbers, Custer ordered an attack. A Native American force numbering between 1,000 and 1,800 warriors wiped out Custer and his 267 men in less than an hour.

Crazy Horse

Crazy Horse, another important Sioux leader, had long studied how the U.S. Army fought. He used his knowledge at both the Rosebud Creek fight and the Battle of the Greasy Grass.

Gall

Sioux leader and warrior Gall (Pizi in the Lakota language) spotted Custer's main force. Together with Crazy Horse, he forced the soldiers into a position where it would be easier for the native warriors to defeat them.

Wovoka's Vision

In 1889, a man named Wovoka, a member of the Paiute tribe, claimed to have a vision. In the vision, Wovoka saw a world of peace and love where people rejoined their dead loved ones and Indians lived as they had before whites arrived. The Sioux also came to believe that in the world Wovoka predicted the bison herds wiped out by white hunters would again roam the Plains.

Wovoka means "woodcutter" in the Northern Paiute language.

As a teenager, Wovoka lived with a white family and used the name Jack Wilson.

The Sioux believed the shirt they wore in the Ghost Dance turned away bullets.

The Ghost Dance is a "round dance," performed in a circle.

Ghost Dancers

The way to bring about this world, Wovoka said, was to live right, avoid violence, and perform a new **ritual** called the Ghost Dance. The Ghost Dance spread through the West. Kicking Bear, a holy man, brought it to the Sioux reservations. Sitting Bull allowed the dancing when he saw his people feared being left out if the vision came true. He worried, however, that soldiers might break up the dance, as they had in other places.

Because the Ghost Dance bonded different peoples together, the army feared it would one day cause Native Americans to rise up and fight again. A respected chief like Sitting Bull might even lead them. On December 15, 1890, a government official ordered Indian police officers to arrest Sitting Bull at his log cabin on the Standing Rock Reservation. A scuffle followed. Sitting Bull was killed.

Sitting Bull (left) refused to surrender to U.S. Army soldiers.

Black Elk had fought in the Battle of the Little Bighorn at age 12.

The bodies of Sioux warriors wrapped in blankets lie in the snow at the site of the Massacre at Wounded Knee.

The Massacre at Wounded Knee

The army then rode to the Pine Ridge Reservation to disarm the Sioux. Near Wounded Knee Creek, the army surrounded a group of Sioux Ghost Dancers. When a deaf Sioux refused to give up his rifle—perhaps because he had not heard the order—shots rang out. After a brief fight, the outgunned Sioux fled. Many were shot as they ran. At least 153 Sioux were killed. "A people's dream died there," the holy man Black Elk said.

Many Plains Indians, including the Cheyenne and Sioux, practiced the Sun Dance ceremonies in structures such as this one.

CHAPTER 4

How the Sioux Lived

Long before the Ghost Dancers, the Sioux had a complicated religion with many beliefs and rituals. The Sioux, in fact, were the first to dance the Sun Dance, a sacred ceremony that spread to almost all Plains peoples. The Sun Dance took place under a full moon early in the summer. For three days, the Sioux danced and prayed. They would **fast** (not eat) during this period to become more pure.

← The Sioux used the phrase "dance looking at the sun."

The Sioux consider the Black Hills sacred.

Vision Quest

Sioux spent the year before a Sun Dance preparing through prayer and a vision quest. During a vision quest, a young man went alone into the wild. Often he journeyed to high, empty places the Sioux believed to be holy, such as the Black Hills. Many vision quests and other ceremonies took place in the Black Hills.

The young man fasted and walked for four days. On his quest he expected to see a guardian spirit in his dreams. The spirit would tell the Sioux what path to take in life. When the young man returned from his vision quest, a holy man explained the vision. He then became the **apprentice** of an older Sioux man and learned the skill revealed to him by his guardian spirit.

On vision quests, spirits often appeared in animal form.

Sioux holy men helped cure sicknesses and interpreted the visions of others.

The Tatanka

When the Sioux became nomads, they took up a life that depended on the *tatanka*—what we call the bison—for food and clothing. At one time at least 30 million bison roamed the Great Plains. A large male stood 6 feet 5 inches (200 centimeters) tall, weighed 1,800 pounds (800 kilograms) or more, and ran 30 miles per hour (50 kilometers per hour). Sioux could harvest about 800 pounds (360 kg) of meat from an adult male.

Both male and female bison have horns.

The Sioux did not have metal tools before Europeans arrived.

A Sioux woman dries meat in the sun.

The Sioux dried bison meat so that it would last and feed them over long distances. Bison, however, provided more than meat. The hide, or skin, was turned into a cover for teepees or became clothing. Bones and horns were carved into tools and knives. Bison were so important that during the 1800s, the U.S. Army slaughtered the animals to starve the Sioux into giving up. Only about 325 bison were still alive by the end of the the 1880s.

Buffalo Jumps

Before horses changed Sioux life, Sioux hunted bison on foot with bows and short spears. One favorite hunting method was to use what is called a buffalo jump. A Sioux community herded bison into lanes with rocks stacked on either side. Once the animals were trapped in a lane, the Sioux stampeded them off a cliff. At the bottom, other Sioux processed the animals for meat, skins, and other useful parts.

Buffalo jumps took place for at least 10,000 years.

A Sioux Timeline

1730
Sioux trade with other native groups and European settlers for horses.

1851
The first Fort Laramie Treaty is signed.

36

The Teepee

The horse allowed the Sioux to follow the bison farther, stampede them more easily, and track down animals when they ran away. Once on horseback, the Sioux became true nomads. Their main form of house, the teepee, was a good fit for their lifestyle. A teepee required just three or four poles and a cover of bison skins sewn together. Sioux women could take it down or put it up in minutes.

1890
The Wounded Knee Massacre occurs.

1875–1876
The Great Sioux War is fought.

Comfort

A well-built teepee kept the people inside warm and dry through the brutal Plains winters. The teepee's design allowed for a fire, because smoke could escape through a hole in the roof. Linings made of decorated bison skins kept cold air out. Rainwater, meanwhile, ran off the teepee's sides. Sioux set up beds around the edges of the teepee and sat against backrests made of woven tree branches.

Willow was a favorite tree for making backrests.

Teepees kept the Sioux warm and dry.

Helpful Plants

Though the Sioux depended on bison, they also used a great many wild plants for food. In the summer and fall, for example, women and children went in search of Plains plants such as wild onions and peas, and fruits such as grapes and strawberries. Other plants served as medicine. Sioux sick with a cold burned leaves from the red cedar tree and breathed the smoke. Children ate milkweed to give them a better appetite.

Milkweed

The Bison Business

Starting in the 1800s, the Sioux killed bison not just for their own use but to sell the hides for money. That allowed them to buy items they could not make themselves, such as guns and metal pans. This also changed Sioux life. Hunting became less of a community event. Instead, individual males hunted to gain wealth and respect. The families of skilled hunters became richer than others, though gift giving made things more equal.

Native Americans used bows and arrows to hunt bison even after they had guns, because they were lighter and easier to reload.

The Pine Ridge Reservation has its own radio station. ➤

The Pine Ridge Reservation in South Dakota is home to about 40,000 people.

Sioux Life Today

Today, the Sioux live on reservations in North and South Dakota, Minnesota, Montana, and Nebraska. There are also reservations in the Canadian provinces of Manitoba and Saskatchewan. Many Sioux remain poor. Jobs are particularly hard to find. On some reservations, 8 in 10 people are unemployed during the winter. In the poorest areas, 7 out of 10 children live in **poverty**. Diabetes and other illnesses are common. Important institutions such as libraries, airports, hospitals, and banks are far away.

One Sioux group hopes to create an independent country.

Sioux women take part in a powwow on the Pine Ridge Reservation.

The Sioux nonetheless work to restore their **traditions** and culture. A group called the Lakota Language Consortium works to teach Sioux children their native language starting in preschool. In 1991, the Akta Lakota Museum and Cultural Center opened to showcase Sioux art and history. A school nearby hosts a Sioux festival of dance and song—called a powwow—every fall. With the Sioux population growing again, it may be that better times are ahead. ★

Year Sioux first traded for horses: Around 1730

Percentage of Native Americans killed in a smallpox outbreak: 80 to 90 percent

Amount the United States paid France for the Louisiana Territory: About $15 million

Length of the Oregon Trail: 2,000 mi. (3,200 km)

Payment agreed to in first Fort Laramie Treaty: $50,000 per year

Number of Native American warriors at Little Bighorn: Between 1,000 and 1,800

Amount of meat taken from a large bison: About 800 lbs. (360 kg)

Number of Sioux deaths at Wounded Knee: At least 153

Did you find the truth?

T The Sioux believed the shirt they wore in the Ghost Dance turned away bullets.

F The Sioux never encountered the Lewis and Clark expedition.

Resources

Books

Birchfield, D. L. *Crazy Horse*. Portsmouth, NH: Heinemann, 2003.

Burgan, Michael. *The Lakota*. New York: Marshall Cavendish, 2008.

Collier, James Lincoln. *The Sitting Bull You Never Knew*. Danbury, CT: Children's Press, 2004.

Englar, Mary. *The Sioux and Their History*. Minneapolis: Compass Point, 2005.

Nelson, S. D. *Black Elk's Vision: A Lakota Story*. New York: Abrams, 2010.

Roop, Peter, and Connie Roop. *Sitting Bull*. New York: Scholastic, 2002.

Waldman, Neil. *Wounded Knee*. New York: Atheneum, 2001.

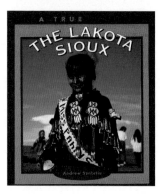

Organizations and Web Sites

Little Bighorn Battlefield National Monument

www.nps.gov/libi/index.htm
Find out the details of the famous battle and look at a webcam showing where it took place at this site from the National Park Service.

South Dakota State Historical Society

http://history.sd.gov/museum
Learn how the Lakota Sioux fit into the history of South Dakota.

Places to Visit

Akta Lakota Museum and Cultural Center

St. Joseph's Indian School
1301 North Main Street
Chamberlain, SD 57325
(800) 798-3452
www.aktalakota.org
Take a journey through Lakota Sioux history and see art created by Lakota artists today.

Buechel Memorial Lakota Museum

350 South Oak Street
P.O. Box 499
St. Francis, SD 57572-0499
(800) 808-8730
www.sfmissionmuseum.org/exhibits
Learn about Lakota culture—including games and how they made bows and arrows—at this museum.

Important Words

apprentice (uh-PREN-tiss) — someone who learns a skill from an expert

cavalry (KAV-uhl-ree) — soldiers mounted on horseback

fast (FAST) — to not eat for a long period of time

hostile (HOS-tuhl) — resisting or acting like an enemy

migrate (MYE-grate) — to move from one place to another

nomads (NOH-madz) — people who move from place to place

poverty (POV-ver-tee) — a state of being poor

reservations (rez-ur-VAY-shuhnz) — land set aside for use by Native Americans

ritual (RICH-oo-uhl) — a religious ceremony with specific rules

sacred (SAY-krid) — having to do with religion or something holy

traditions (truh-DISH-uhnz) — patterns of thought or action passed down from generation to generation

treaty (TREE-tee) — an agreement or deal that is legally binding on the two or more groups who sign

Index

Page numbers in **bold** indicate illustrations

About the Authors

Kevin Cunningham has written more than 40 books on disasters, the history of disease, Native Americans, and other topics. Cunningham lives near Chicago with his wife and young daughter.

Peter Benoit is educated as a mathematician but has many other interests. He has taught and tutored high school and college students for many years, mostly in math and science. He also runs summer workshops for writers and students of literature. Benoit has written more than 2,000 poems. His life has been one committed to learning. He lives in Greenwich, New York.